100 Questions and Answers About Indian Americans

A Guide in Cultural Competence

Michigan State University School of Journalism

Read The Spirit Books

an imprint of
David Crumm Media, LLC
Canton, Michigan

For more information and further discussion, visit
news.jrn.msu.edu/culturalcompetence/

Cover art and design by
Rick Nease
www.RickNeaseArt.com

Series Editor: Joe Grimm

Published By
Read The Spirit Books
an imprint of
David Crumm Media, LLC
42015 Ford Rd., Suite 234
Canton, Michigan, USA

For information about customized editions, bulk pur-
chases or permissions, contact David Crumm Media,
LLC at info@DavidCrummMedia.com

Contents

About this guide

THIS GUIDE IS part of the Michigan State University School of Journalism series in cultural competence. It is intended to be a brief introduction, just a slim beginning. We intend this guide as a starting point that leads to other people and resources.

The guide is intended for people in business, schools, places of worship, government, medicine, law enforcement and journalism—anywhere it is important to know more about communities. We hope this guide works for individuals who just have questions about the people around them.

We began by asking Indian Americans about myths, misconceptions and biases that they run into and wish others knew more about. We then set out to answer those questions. Finally, we sorted the questions into chapters and asked members of the community to check our work.

Many people graciously helped. We thank Vikas Bajaj of The New York Times, Padma Kuppa of the Hindu American Foundation, Krishnan Anantharaman of Automotive News, Neal Justin of the Minneapolis Star Tribune, Jewel Gopwani of the Detroit Free Press, John Golaszewski of the Michigan Department of Civil Rights, Pam Bolden of Consumers Energy, Lucinda Davenport, director of the MSU School of Journalism and John Hile of David Crumm Media.

The guide was created by MSU journalism students Dmitri Barvinok, Celeste Bott, Marisol Dorantes, George Farmer, Alyssa Firth, Carly Hill, Rikki Jarvis, Aaron Jordan, Max King, Richard Kuhn, Devyne Lloyd, Marissa Russo and Hayley Shannon.

This guide is published by David Crumm Media.

Joe Grimm is the series editor. He takes responsibility for any omissions, errors or oversights. Please direct questions and concerns to him at joe.grimm@gmail.com.

CHAPTER **1**

History

1. What makes Indians Asian?

India is part of the Asian continent. It has historically been geographically divided from the rest of Asia by two mountain ranges, the Hindu Kush and the Himalayas, formed from tectonic action between the Indian plate and the Asian one.

2. What are the other countries of South Asia?

The United Nations classifies South Asia as Bangladesh, Bhutan, India, Maldives, Nepal, Pakistan and Sri Lanka.

3. What race are Indians?

Racial classification in India is difficult. The government discourages classifying people according to racial distinctions and the census there does not gather that information. Anthropologists classify Indians from the north, south, northeast and southeast parts of the country as belonging to different racial or ethnic groups. Intermarriage makes distinctions less clear.

4. Why are some Indians so dark and others aren't?

Skin color and genetics has been shown scientifically to change in any given geographic area. It is simply a fact of people with a diverse gene pool followed by natural and cultural selection.

5. How old is India?

Humans and their predecessors have lived in what we now call India for thousands of years. The area had many kingdoms and political entities. In the 1600s, Britain's East India Trade Company began acquiring more influence in the subcontinent and this led to foreign rule. British rule of the region from 1858 to 1947 was called the British Raj. When the British left, the country was partitioned into India and Pakistan. On Aug. 14, 1947, Pakistan achieved independence, and India became independent the next day. In 1971 Pakistan split, with the eastern part of the country becoming the country of Bangladesh.

6. Why are there tensions between Pakistan and India?

Pakistan was created as a Muslim-majority country separate from India, which is dominated by Hindus and has large minorities of Muslims, Sikhs and followers of other religions. The separation of the two countries, known as the partition, resulted in violent riots as people were uprooted. Many Muslims moved from what is now India to

Pakistan and many Hindus moved from what is now Pakistan to India. About 500,000 people died. Conflict still exists over governance of Jammu and Kashmir, a once autonomous state. Many Pakistanis believe it should be part of Pakistan because of its predominantly Muslim population. India states that it belongs to India because it agreed to join the country in 1947.

7. Who was Gandhi?

Mohandas Gandhi is considered the father of the Indian independence movement. Gandhi spent 20 years in South Africa working to fight discrimination. There, he developed the philosophy of satyagraha, a non-violent way of protesting injustice. Upon his return to India, he took up the cause of opposing British rule. Using civil disobedience, he led India to independence and inspired movements for non-violence, civil rights and freedom throughout the world. Gandhi is popularly known as "Mahatma," which means great soul. Indira Gandhi was prime minister of India from 1966 to 1977 and from 1980 until her assassination in 1984. The two are not related.

CHAPTER 2

Population

8. How many Indians are there?

India is the second most populous country in the world with more than 1.2 billion people. It is projected to overtake China. India has four times as many people as the United States. Its land area is roughly the same as 40 percent of the United States without Alaska and Hawaii.

9. How many live in the United States?

The U.S. Census Bureau reported in 2010 that there were 3,183,063 Indians in America, about 1 percent of the U.S. population. Of those, the bureau estimated in 2011 that approximately 1,857,000 were born in India. Most Indians immigrate legally and in numbers set by U.S. policy, which raised the limit in 1965.

10. How long have Indians been in the United States?

Indians have been in the United States for more than 100 years, but entrance to the United States was restricted for a long time. The Immigration and Nationality Act of 1965 replaced a national origins quota system with a system based on skills and people's relationships to U.S. citizens and residents. The old system had limited Asian and African immigration. The Pew Research Center reports that 87 percent of Indians in America over the age of 18 were born outside the United States. As a group, Indians are younger than the U.S. average. U.S. demand for highly skilled workers has increased Indian immigration.

11. Where do Indians in the United States primarily live?

Indians live in all 50 U.S. states, with about a third concentrated in the Northeast. According to the U.S. Census Bureau, states with the most India-born residents are California (381,000), New Jersey (210,000), Texas (162,000), New York (145,000) and Illinois (127,000). Indians are one of the largest immigrant groups in the United States.

12. What brings them to the United States?

The two main drivers of immigrants to the United States from other countries tend to be opportunity and security. Most Indians come here for educational or employment opportunity. Many Indians who end up staying in the U.S. start out as graduate students in science, information technology and engineering programs. Emigration from India and foreign education can be signs of prestige.

13. What are wages like in India?

The CIA World Factbook estimated the 2012 Gross Domestic Product per person for India was $3,900, compared to $49,800 for the United States. There is a vast wage disparity in India, where there are professionals, entrepreneurs, government workers and many people in low-paying jobs.

14. Do immigrants come from a particular part of India?

The first Indian immigrants to the United States came from the Punjab region. Today, Indians represent many regions, languages and cultural groups. Many do not come from India at all. Communities exist all over the world, so about 20 percent of Indians in America were born outside of India. Of U.S. Indians, about 4 percent come from Guyana and British Guyana, 2 percent came here from Pakistan or Trinidad and Tobago and another 1 percent come from Bangladesh and the United Kingdom. They also come to the United States from Canada and through Mexico.

15. What kind of communities do Indians come from?

Indians live in the country, on the coasts and in cities. India's largest city, Mumbai, formerly Bombay, is the financial capital and has 12.5 million people. Delhi has 11 million. Bangalore has more than 8 million and is about the size of New York City. Other major cities are Kolkata and Chennai.

While the U.S. had nine cities with populations of more than 1 million in 2011, India had 46.

16. Why did Mumbai and Delhi change their names?

The renaming of some Indian cities and states began with the end of Imperial British rule in 1947. A 1956 reorganization of states, changes to local languages and differences between Indian and British English caused more. Changes continue. Locals may say New Delhi for the planned capital city developed by the British shortly before independence, and "Old Delhi" for the historic capital of the many empires that ruled there. However, "Delhi" is also the shorthand name of an administrative unit—officially the National Capital Territory of Delhi—that encompasses both the old and new sections. Other changes:

- Bombay became Mumbai, as it's known in the local Marathi language.
- Bangalore became Bengaluru, as it's known in Kannada, the local language.
- Calcutta became Kolkata, as it's known in Bengali, the local language.
- Madras, the city, became Chennai, as it's known in Tamil. Madras, the state, became Tamil Nadu (literally "Tamil-land").
- Cochin became Kochi, as it's known in Malayalam, the local language.

- Trivandrum became Thiruvananthapuram. This is from Sanskrit, a root language of Malayalam and other languages.

17. We hear a lot about Bangalore. Why?

Bangalore is called the Silicon Valley of India for its entrepreneurship and information technology. It is mentioned frequently in conversations about offshoring.

18. What is the caste system?

This was India's system of social hierarchy. At its root, it was a system referred to in Hindu scriptures that aimed to classify people based on their nature, aptitude and conduct, and put them to work in functions that suited their classification. Later interpretations resulted in a hereditary and hierarchical structure that was the basis for centuries of segregation and discrimination in traditional communities. It sharply limited socioeconomic mobility. Changes in the law since independence have removed many vestiges of caste-based discrimination. However, it persists in many traditional villages and communities. Caste also forms the basis for a range of quotas and affirmative-action policies enacted by the Indian government aimed at erasing the legacy of discrimination in higher education and government employment. In many instances, these quotas and preferences have exacerbated tensions and resentments between caste groups and deepened caste-based identity and prejudice. Communities or castes can discourage marrying, associating or even dining with people of other groups. Indians in the United States do not use a caste system and freedom from it may encourage immigration.

CHAPTER 3

Religion

19. What religion do Indians practice?

India is the birthplace to four of the world's major religions: Hinduism, Buddhism, Sikhism and Jainism. Indians practice many more, but the largest by far is Hinduism. 2001 Indian census data shows about 80 percent of the population in India is Hindu. Other religions include Islam (13.4 percent), Christianity (2.3 percent), Sikhism (1.9 percent), Buddhism (.8 percent) and Jainism (.4 percent). Zoroastrianism, Judaism, the Baha'i Faith and other religions are also practiced. Some Indians are atheists. Christianity has been practiced by the Mar Thoma Nasrani church for more than 1,500 years.

20. What is the role of religion in Indian society?

India's constitution declares the nation to be a secular republic that upholds the right of citizens to freely worship and propagate any religion or faith. In practice, religious divisions have served as fault lines in Indian society. According to the Pew

Research Center, one-third of Indians feel that the United States has greater religious freedom than India.

21. What is the religious picture for Indians in the United States?

Communities of Hindus, Muslims, Christians, Sikhs, Jains, Buddhists, Parsis and Jews from India practice their religions in the United States. According to a 2012 study by the Pew Research Center, 51 percent consider themselves Hindu, 18 percent Christian (Protestant 11 percent, Catholic 5 percent, other Christian 3 percent), 10 percent Muslim, 5 percent Sikh, 2 percent Jain and 10 percent are unaffiliated. India's traditional religions are also practiced by non-Indian Americans. The Hindu American Foundation estimates the Hindu population of America at 2 million and estimates that 32 million others are inspired by Hindu spirituality. In Canada, there are more Sikhs than Hindus and that plays a role in the religion's development in the United States.

22. What is Hinduism?

Hinduism is a system of beliefs, values and customs that have grown out of Sanatana Dharma, or "the eternal law," as described in ancient scriptures known as the Vedas. Underlying this system is a belief in "Brahman" (rhymes with Grumman)—also referred to as "the Self" or "Supreme Self'" or "God"—as an indivisible, indestructible, unchanging, perpetual and all-encompassing force that binds all living things and the universe together. The purpose of life, according to this belief, is "self-realization," to liberate oneself from the temporal, world of desires and pleasures as experienced by the sense organs; from emotional ups and downs; and from the cycle of life and death, and to recognize our oneness with the divine force—essentially to become one with God. The scriptures describe three main paths to self-realization—selfless action, the acquisition of knowledge, and devotion—but leave it to individuals to follow the path and combination that best fits their temperament, circumstances and station in life. Hindus believe that we remain in this cycle of birth and death—reincarnation—until we attain self-realization.

23. Do Hindus believe in multiple gods?

Hindus worship one supreme being but a trinity of gods: Brahma, Vishnu and Shiva. The Vedas, the sacred scriptures for Hindus, says there is one truth and that the wise call it by many names. In the Rig Veda alone – one of the four sacred texts of Hinduism – there are 33 gods. Some scholars say there are millions of Hindu deities, and that the multitude signifies the infinite forms of one god. Some of the deities have fanciful shapes. Although Hindus build temples, much of their worship occurs at home altars.

24. Do Hindus worship cows?

No. Hindus respect and honor the cow because all living things are sacred, but they do not worship cows in the sense that they worship God. Symbolically, the cow is a generous sustainer of life that provides milk and helps plough with crops, but that takes nothing other than what is necessary for its own sustenance. It is respected for this.

25. What is the dot that some people wear on their foreheads?

The dot is a bindi, or bindhi, a Hindi word for the decoration traditionally worn on the forehead of married Hindu women. It symbolizes female energy and is believed to protect women and their husbands. Culturally, the bindi accentuates the third eye, where attention is focused during meditation, or a point of concealed wisdom. Traditionally, the bindi was red. More recently, the bindi has become worn as a decorative accessory by unmarried girls and non-Hindu women. It is also no longer restricted in color or shape. Jewelry and self-adhesive bindis made of felt in various designs and colors are being worn.

26. Do Muslims have much influence in India?

Even though Muslims are less than 20 percent of India's population, 177 million adherents make India the third largest Muslim country in the world by population. Indonesia is the largest and

Pakistan has slightly more Muslims than India. Islam is the world's second largest religion behind Christianity. Hinduism is the world's third largest religion.

27. Are Sikhs the same as Muslims?

No. Sikhism is a separate religion founded by Guru Nanak in India's Punjab region. Sikhs, which means students or disciples, believe in one God and pursue salvation by the name and message of God as revealed by a succession of 10 gurus who lived from about 1470 to 1709. In a little more than 500 years, Sikhism has become the fifth largest religion in the world. Sikhism stresses equality and rejects discrimination based on gender, caste or creed.

28. What is a guru?

Guru means teacher. The term is used in the major Indian religions of Hinduism, Sikhism and Buddhism. In popular English, it means any sort of knowledgeable guide or mentor.

29. What do Jains believe?

Jainism is one of the oldest religions in the world. It teaches that non-violence and self-control free people from the cycle of reincarnation. Jains believe in spiritual independence and equality among all forms of life. Non-violence is a core value for Jains and extends to diet, which is strictly vegetarian and includes fasting. Jains have ancient and extensive religious texts. They pray to escape worldly desires for the liberation of their souls.

30. What are some major religious holidays that Indians celebrate in America?

Indians observe various holidays because they are a diverse group and practice many religions. Christian Indians, for example, celebrate Christmas. Indians also celebrate non-religious holidays, as other Americans do, for occasions such as independence or harvest time. Major religious festivals practiced by some religions include the Festival of Lights and Ganesh Chaturthi.

31. What is the Festival of Lights?

Also known as Diwali, the festival of lights is a five-day celebration of the triumph of good over evil. It is celebrated by Hindus, Sikhs and Jains. Diwali or Divali is a contraction of Deepavali, which means "row of lamps." Originally associated with harvest season, Diwali can include the lighting of small clay lamps. These lamps are kept on during the night and one's house is cleaned to welcome Lakshmi, the goddess of prosperity, wealth, purity, generosity. Diwali is also celebrated with strings of lights, fireworks and gifts. Diwali is celebrated on a lunar calendar, so the dates change from years to year on the Gregorian calendar commonly used in America.

32. And holidays for Muslim Indians?

Two major holidays for Muslims everywhere are the month of fasting called Ramadan and its conclusion, Eid Al-Fitr. Another is Eid al-Adha. This four-day observance commemorates the willingness of the prophet Abraham to sacrifice his first-born son, Ishmael. God intervened and substituted a lamb for Ishmael.

33. Is Hare Krishna an Indian religion?

The International Society for Krishna Consciousness was founded in 1966 in New York City. A. C. Bhaktivedanta Swami Prabhupada, its founder, based it on traditional Indian scriptures. The consciousness promotes bhakti yoga, in which people dedicate their thoughts and actions toward pleasing the deity Supreme Lord Krishna. Members are known for chanting their mantra in public places.

CHAPTER 4

Language

34. What language do people speak in India?

India has 14 officially recognized languages. In addition there are many more fully developed languages. They are distinct and are not merely separate dialects of the same language, although there are many dialects, too. India's 2001 census found 29 languages with 1 million or more native speakers. The most prevalent, Hindi, was spoken by more than 40 percent of Indians. The next seven languages by popularity were Bengali, Telugu, Marathi, Tamil, Urdu, Guajarathi and Kannada. Combined, those languages were used by another 40 percent of Indians.

35. With so many languages, how do people communicate?

Language is very political in India. Many state borders are drawn on the basis of language, so within states, people generally speak the same language. Among people who are from different language groups, Hindi and English are the most common link languages. English is used for government business. Many Indians use two or three or more languages.

36. So, Hindi is the language and Hindu is the religion?

Pretty much. Use Hindu to identify someone who practices Hinduism, which is not just the religion, but a broad and diverse historical and cultural identity. The language is Hindi, a shortened form of Hindustani, meaning "of the land of Hindus." Not all Hindus speak Hindi.

37. What is Sanskrit?

Sanskrit is one of the oldest languages in the world that is still being used. It is the root for many other languages. They include Hindi, Punjabi, Tamil, Telugu, Kannada, Malayalam, Marathi, Oriya, Bengali, Gujarati and Nepali. Sanskrit literature often consists of poetry, philosophical, and dharma texts. It is widely used for religion and ceremony.

38. Are Indian languages written down?

Most are. Sanskrit is known for its precise alphabet, compact writing system and complex grammar rules. Some, but not all, Sanskrit-based languages use the Devanagari script or variations of it. The more stylized ones are Bengali and Gujarati.

39. Where do most Indians learn English?

In school. Remember that British India lasted until August 1947, so English has been common for some time. Most educated Indians learn English and use it to conduct business.

40. Can Indian children in America speak a native Indian language?

Many second-generation Indian-Americans understand an Indian language and might speak it, but are often unable to write or read it.

41. What does Desi mean?

Desi (THEY-see) comes from Sanskrit and means, "from the country" or "of the country." It implies shared values or bonds.

42. And what is an ABCD?

It means "American Born Confused Desi" and many consider it to be a slur. It refers to children of Indian immigrants in the United States. The expression comes from the cultural adjustment that the second generation might experience when dealing with an Indian culture at home and American culture outside the home. The term can echo derogatory terms applied to other immigrants and should not be used loosely or carelessly.

43. I have heard people called by terms like Ji and Sri. What do they mean?

Ji and Sri are, among some Indians, terms of respect. A name for father is baba or babu. Babuji shows respect to one's father. Sri, coming before a man's name, is like saying "mister." Of course, auntie and uncle are used in many cultures. Do not presume to know when it is appropriate to use a familiar term of address. It can be informative to ask their meanings when you hear them.

44. What do Apna and Apni mean?

Apna is slang and means "one's own" people. It refers to a male of the same race. Apni is the equivalent for females.

CHAPTER 5

Culture

45. What is a sari?

This garment is essentially a piece of fabric generally six yards long that is wrapped around the body. It is generally wrapped around the waist and draped over the shoulder, leaving the midriff bare. Types of fabric, styles and prices vary. A sari is sometimes worn with a blouse.

46. Why do Indians wear turbans?

People wear turbans for different reasons, and there are different types of turbans. Sikh men wear turbans that peak at the forehead to take care of their hair, which they do not cut, and to promote equality among themselves and to declare their identity. Turbans make Sikhs distinctive in India, where they are a minority. In the United States, Sikhs have been attacked by people who assumed the turbans meant they were Muslims. Most Muslims do not wear turbans, though their religious leaders might wear one. It's typically spherical or conical. The shape of those turbans varies by country. Men also wear turbans for reasons having nothing to do with religion.

47. Is yoga Indian?

Yes. It began as a meditative process. Today, there are many kinds of yoga. In yoga, one controls breath, heart rate and consciousness to achieve a meditative state. It also uses concentration and practiced breathing. In western nations, yoga is often done more as a form of exercise. There has been controversy when yoga based in spirituality has been introduced in public schools.

48. Why do Indian people have such long names?

Not all Indian surnames are long. Some are short. Some appear long when transliterated into Roman script. Some Indian names, like European names, are occupational or indicate kinship or place of origin. Others refer to God in different ways and are what might seem in English to be short sentences.

49. Why is the name Patel so common?

This surname is used so frequently that some people refer to Indians as Patels, an insulting generality. The Patel name occurs frequently in the state of Gujarat in north India, though it also occurs in other states and major cities. Immigration patterns can increase its frequency in U.S. communities.

50. What is Bollywood?

Bollywood is the Indian movie industry's equivalent of Hollywood. It is a popular term for Hindi cinema. Bollywood is not the only source of Indian cinema and movies are made in other languages, but Bollywood is the largest. Bollywood movies have been through several genres, but they are often musicals with singing and dancing.

51. Where is Bollywood?

Although Hollywood has a sign on a hillside, Bollywood is not a specific place. The name is a combination of Bombay, the city now called Mumbai, and Hollywood. Bollywood is a vast pop culture industry. It is the largest producer of movies in the world, ahead of Hollywood and France. Bollywood's influence is showing up more in U.S. theaters, music and on television shows like "Dancing with the Stars."

52. Did the movie "Slumdog Millionaire" portray India accurately?

The 2008 movie about an orphaned street child who wins a quiz show is, by definition, fantasy. In some ways it symbolizes India's rise from poverty. Some Indians, however, said it made too much of poverty and street crime. One critic wrote that its portrayal of poverty was little better than a snake-charmer stereotype. The movie uses English and Hindi and has a rags-to-riches theme.

53. What is the snake-charmer stereotype?

In several Asian and African countries, snake charmers have entranced audiences and tourists by appearing to hypnotize snakes with an instrument like a flute. The practice, which was not that common, is being eclipsed by other entertainment. As portrayed in American movies and cartoons, it made India seem exotic and backward.

54. What are the East Indies and West Indies?

The West Indies are a group of islands in the Caribbean Sea that includes Puerto Rico, Cuba and the Bahamas. They acquired that name because Spanish explorers erroneously thought they had sailed to India. Europeans had earlier labeled South Asia as the "East Indies" after the Indus River.

55. The terms Bengali and Bangladeshi are confusing. Is there a difference?

Yes, Bengal is a very populous region on the eastern part of the subcontinent along the Bay of Bengal. During the Partition of 1947, which created independent India and Pakistan, Bengal was split along religious lines. The western part, which was mostly Hindu, became a state in India called West Bengal. The eastern part, mostly Muslim, became East Pakistan—part of the single nation, Pakistan, that was split between two non-contiguous areas. Following a civil war (in which India supported the Bengali insurgents against Pakistani government forces), East Pakistan became an independent country in 1971, called Bangladesh, or "Bengal Country." By language and ethnicity, people in both West Bengal and Bangladesh are Bengali; they are part of the same region. But by nationality, people from Bangladesh are called Bangladeshis.

56. What is henna?

Henna is a plant used to make ink or hair dye. To make the ink, leaves are ground to powder and mixed with water and lemon juice or oil. The ceremonial application of henna to make designs on the body, usually hands or feet, is called mehndi. Indian women wear mehndi for special occasions such as weddings. The designs start to fade after about a week.

57. Why is red popular in Indian culture?

Red is the good-luck color in several cultures, including Indian and Chinese. It is a favored color for weddings in both cultures and it the traditional color for the bindi worn by Indian women. Although red is the most popular color for national flags, it is not in the Indian flag.

58. Are Indians non-athletic?

This stereotype is used on people of all Asian origins. British rule influenced Indian sports from before the time when America's major sports were created. Top sports in India include cricket, soccer (called football), and badminton, which was invented there. India dominated Olympic field hockey competition from 1928 to 1980, winning eight gold medals. Other popular sports for Indians include basketball, golf and tennis. Historically, malnutrition has played a role in limiting Indians' success in competitive athletics, and the national government does not invest heavily in resources for athletic training or facilities. Also, India does not have a well-developed system of interscholastic or intercollegiate sports to help develop internationally competitive athletes, so sports have not been seen as a pathway to success as much as academic competition. Many Indian Olympians have come from the ranks of the army or police forces, where fitness training is more intense. Indians who grow up in America play sports that are popular here. Professional Indian athletes in the United States have included football players Brandon Chillar and Bobby Singh, hockey player Manny Malhotra and gymnast Raj Bhavsar.

CHAPTER 6

Food

59. Are Indians vegetarians?

Many are, but not all. There are different degrees of vegetarianism and different reasons for its practice. Some Indian vegetarians are also vegan but others might drink milk and eat eggs. Some are vegetarian for religious reasons. Jainism and Buddhism teach nonviolence and balance with the universe, so meat and animal by-products are forbidden. Hindu and Muslim diets exclude certain animals. Other people are vegetarian for financial reasons. Meat is expensive. Roughly 30 to 40 percent of the people in India are vegetarians. Food that is vegetarian-safe is labeled with a green dot in a green square. In India, the McDonald's restaurant chain sells the McAlooTikki, its interpretation of India's aloo tikki, a potato patty with spices.

60. Is Indian food hot and spicy?

It can be, although geographic, cultural and religious variations give India many cuisines. Many Indian recipes call for chilies and other spices that add heat or flavor to a dish. Most Indian restaurants in the United States serve American-ized dishes or concentrate on north Indian cuisine, which is less spicy than that from the south. Indian food is served around the world.

61. What is curry?

Curry refers to either dishes or spice mixes. A curry dish refers to meat, fish, vegetables or a combination of those cooked with spices and served in a gravy or dry. Curry can also refer to a blend of spices, herbs and usually chilies. One of those spices can be made from the leaves of the curry tree. Others might include ginger, cardamom, saffron, coriander, cinnamon, turmeric, asafoetida, cumin and black pepper. Curries can be hot, mild or sweet and are made in several countries. Curry powder, as packaged for U.S. grocery stores, is a largely western concoction. There is not a singularly authentic version of curry.

62. Why are Indians associated with curry?

As we just read, curry is used in many places. However, some people use references to curry to insult Indians. There is a history in the United States of saying foods from other countries are strange or objectionable. It has happened to Italians, Koreans, Somalis and others. This is done to ostracize people and to imply that their food and, by extension, they, do not belong.

63. What is the connection between India and tea?

The British East India Tea Company, eager for an alternative to Chinese suppliers, introduced tea cultivation in India in the early 1800s. Indians did not become big tea drinkers until an advertising blitz by the India Tea Board in the 1950s.

64. What are Assam and Darjeeling teas?

These teas are named after the regions in northeast India where they were developed and are grown.

65. Why do some Indians fast?

Indians, particularly Hindus, fast to get closer to a spiritual deity. They fast by not eating at all, eating only once a day, or eating a simple diet such as fruit and bread, bread and water or vegetables. Fasting also occurs during or as a precursor to religious festivals and ceremonies. Muslims fast during the month of Ramadan. Jains also fast.

66. Do Indians in America still eat their traditional foods?

Many do and many non-Indians eat Indian foods at restaurants and at home. Assimilation varies for all immigrants and by generation. While many families continue to cook and eat traditional foods, they might add food from America and other cultures. Religion can play a role in this.

CHAPTER 7

Family and gender

67. Are Indian marriages arranged?

In all cultures, parents seem to want to help their children find good mates. A referral or an introduction is not a forced marriage and those have become less common in Indian cities and in the United States, where young adults are more independent. Some reject suggestions entirely. There is a thriving business of matrimonial ads for Indians.

68. Must Indians in America return to India to find or marry a spouse?

No. That is up to the person and the family, but it is not the norm. According to the Pew Research Center, 12 percent of Indian Americans who married in 2008-2010 married non-Asians and 2 percent married non-Indian Asians.

69. Do Indians pay dowries?

The payment of dowry to the husband's family, often financial, has an old history in many parts of the world. India banned dowries in 1961.

70. Do Indians marry young?

The national age for marriage in India is 21 for men and 18 for women. The legal age in the United States is 18 for both. With waivers or permission from judges or guardians, some U.S. states allow marriages by females as young as 13 and males as young as 14. The average age of when people actually marry is rising in both countries.

71. Are Indian weddings really long?

Traditional Hindu weddings can last for days and involve many rituals in Sanskrit, which might be understood only by the priest conducting the service. Ceremonies performed by Indian Americans in the United States are considerably shorter and are designed to be understandable to non-Indian attendees, making it suitable for intercultural or interreligious marriages. Pre-wedding ceremonies include engagement involving oral and written declaration and the arrival of the groom's party at the bride's residence, often in the form of a formal procession. Post-wedding ceremonies involve welcoming the bride to her new home.

72. Do Indian generations live together?

It is not uncommon for generations of Indian families to live together. Loyalty to family is an important ideal in Indian culture, so in many cases several generations of a family may live together and support one another. In cases where an Indian family operates as a nuclear family, relatives might live nearby, but immigration can also mean thousands of miles of distance among family members.

73. Do Indians care for their elders at home?

The Indian tradition is for children to take care of their parents in the home. That is changing, however, even in India, as more senior homes get built and as the stigma eases of having one's parents living in eldercare.

74. How are gender roles treated?

Indian families and society have historically been patriarchal. While laws, education and politics have given women greater equality, male domination is still an issue. The women's rights movement in India has been spurred by violent attacks on women and the legal system's response to them. Discrimination and sex-selective abortions that favor males are also issues in India.

CHAPTER 8

Jobs

75. Why are so many Indians in information technology, engineering and medicine?

That is much truer in the United States than in India. U.S. immigration policies favor highly skilled workers. Most Indians allowed to immigrate into the United States have a bachelor's or master's degree. According to U.S. Census data, 75 percent of Indians in America 20 years and older have a college or professional degree.

76. What other occupations do Indians have?

According to the 2000 census, 25.8 percent of working Indian Americans were involved in science, computers and engineering and 22.5 percent were in sales, operations and support. The next three broad categories were skilled blue collar at 12.4 percent, medical at 11.8 percent and executive jobs at 11.1 percent.

77. Are Indians in America well paid?

Yes. Because advanced degrees are so prevalent among Indians in America, they also earn good wages, on average. According to a 2012 Pew Research Center report, the median household income for Indians was $88,000 compared to $66,000 for all Asians in America and $49,800 for the general population.

78. Is it truth or a stereotype that Indians run a lot of hotels?

It is true. The Asian American Hotel Owners Association reports that half the hotels in the United States are owned by Indians. Many came from Gujarat in the 1960s and 1970s. Entrepreneurship is widespread in that state. Many helped relatives get started in the business, a migration pattern practiced by many nationalities.

79. Is that what the term "Patel motel" refers to?

Yes. Seventy percent of all Indian hotel owners are named Patel, equivalent to a third of all motel owners in America.

80. Are there other occupational stereotypes about Indians?

Yes, and they run in opposite directions. One is that they Indians all work in highly skilled jobs like information technology and engineering.

Other stereotypes say Indians run convenience stores or donut shops or drive taxis and trucks. Indians work in both areas.

81. Why do so many Indians go into business for themselves?

This has been attributed to several reasons. One is that a lack of language fluency, U.S. credentials and prejudice force them to work for themselves. Another is that family networks provide help and capital to help them get started.

82. Why do we import so many Indians in information technology?

Many Asian Indians hired by U.S. companies come here on H1B visas. These 6-year nonimmigrant visas are issued for specialty occupations like engineering and mathematics when no U.S. citizen or resident is found for the job. There are not enough people in America to fill all positions for occupations like information technology, so employers apply for H1B visas to bring people here to fill openings. Indian companies have trouble hiring enough people to do these jobs, too.

83. Do Indians steal American jobs?

Both major parties in the United States have used that line to criticize their political opponents. It is a vast oversimplification. Companies hire foreign workers to save on wages, satisfy consumer demand for bargains, or to solve labor or skills shortages. When you see reports about this issue, see whether the reports indicate how many jobs are generated when immigrants are hired.

84. Why are so many call center workers Indian?

U.S. companies outsource many kinds of jobs to India and other countries, but telemarketing is noticeable because it puts foreign workers and Americans on the phone with each other. India has a large pool of English-speaking workers who want the wages call centers will pay them. In recent years, the Philippines has displaced India as the biggest hub of offshore call centers.

85. Have many American jobs have been outsourced to India?

This is hard to pin down. Sometimes American companies open factories in other countries to be closer to their customers. Sometimes, they move factories overseas and ship products back to the United States. That is called offshoring. When companies hire other firms to do work they used to do, that is called outsourcing. Onshoring is also part of the story. U.S. companies are not required to report these moves, so estimates come from consultants and trade groups. Estimates can be politically motivated, they vary widely and may or may not reflect the number of jobs saved by economizing.

86. What is onshoring?

In this context, onshoring is when a U.S. company hires an international company to create an operation in the United States.

87. Why does onshoring happen?

There are a couple reasons. One is that U.S. companies have found that some high-end work is better performed closer to home. Another is that it is becoming difficult to get as many work visas as companies would like. So, we wind up with an international company setting up shop in the United States. That company might hire foreign and domestic workers.

CHAPTER 9

Education

88. Indians seem to be really smart. Are they?

This is two stereotypes bundled into one. The first is that Indians are good with technology. The second is that people in technology, science and engineering are smarter than others. This much is clear: Indians in the United States have, on average, completed more education than the general population.

89. Why are Indians in America so highly educated?

U.S. immigration policies favor highly skilled adults. The Pew Research Center's Social and Demographic Trends report shows that Indians are one of the most highly educated groups in the U.S. population. While 28 percent of all Americans over the age of 25 have at least a bachelor's degree, the figure for Indians in America is 70 percent.

90. What about advanced degrees?

Pew reports that 38 percent of Indians in America over the age of 25 have master's degrees or higher. Only 10 percent of all Americans have that much education.

91. How is U.S. education different from India's?

With the exception of a few elite institutions, the education system in India is generally weaker than in the U.S. In Indian schools, grades K-12 are known as "standards." In most modern schools, there are two levels of kindergarten, followed by 10 to 12 grades, as in American schools. The final two years, known as higher secondary or "plus two," were once considered part of a college education, but are now mostly included in high school to conform more to international norms. In recent years, enrollment in primary schools has crossed 90 percent, but the quality of education can be weak, especially in government-run schools and in schools in rural areas. A government program to provide free lunches to students and parents' desire to see their children get an education has boosted enrollment. Private schools have been growing fast and even poor parents prefer to send their children to private institutions, some of which charge just a few dollars per month.

92. Is education an important consideration in coming to the United States?

It's very common for Indian students to attend college or graduate school in the United States. Indians are now the second-largest foreign student population in America, after the Chinese, with almost 105,000 students in the United States in the 2009-10 academic year.

93. Why are Indians good at math?

Again, this is a generality. In India, engineering and medicine are desirable professions. Those who pass rigorous entrance exams and attend the right schools for those skills can escape poverty. Millions do not get to take the exams or fail them. When computer-based technology industries expanded in the United States, degrees related to mathematics and engineering became more desirable because they gave Indians the chance to live, work and go to school in the United States.

94. Are Indians good with technology?

According to U.S. Census data, the proportion of Indian adults working in the computer, software and engineering sector in the United States is higher than for any other group. Three quarters of Indians in the United States do not work in technology. Most information technology people are not Indian.

CHAPTER **10**

Politics

95. What political system does India use?

India is the largest democracy in the world. Its
government is similar to Britain's parliamentary
system. It has a bicameral parliament led by the
Lok Sabha, or People's Assembly, and a prime minister who leads the ruling party or coalition and
serves as the head of government. Members of
the Lok Sabha are elected by the people. Members
of the Upper House, or Rajya Sabha, are mostly
elected by state legislatures. India's indirectly
elected president has powers analogous to those of
the queen in the United Kingdom or the governor
general in Canada. India has dozens of second-tier
and local political parties that are represented at
the national level. Individual states have their own
legislative assemblies. Judicial powers are vested
in a Supreme Court as well as several lower circuit
courts called "High Courts."

96. Does India have a king?

No. Years ago, before British India, the subcontinent had many kingdoms and principalities. Some

kings continued to rule under British patrimony, but all such states were absorbed into India or Pakistan after independence.

97. Do women have voting rights in India?

The Indian constitution prohibits discrimination on the basis of religion, race, caste, sex or place of birth. Women were given the right to vote in 1935, 15 years after the United States did. Indira Gandhi, daughter of India's first prime minister, served as prime minister from 1966 to 1977 and 1980 to 1984. Pratibha Patil, a woman, was India's president from 2007 to 2012.

98. Are Indians involved in U.S. politics?

Republican governors Bobby Jindal of Louisiana and Nikki Haley of South Carolina are Indian Americans. Jindal had been considered as a running mate for Gov. Mitt Romney in the 2012 presidential election. Ami Bera, a Democrat from California, is a U.S. congressman. Bera was the third Indian-American to be elected to Congress. Dalip Singh Saund was the first, elected in 1952, and Jindal, elected in 2004, was second. Five other Indian-Americans ran unsuccessfully for Congress in 2012.

99. How do Indians in America vote?

According to the Pew Research Center, about two-thirds of Indian Americans favor Democrats and about 18 percent favor Republicans.

100. Is Indian political influence growing in America?

That seems likely. Because Indian immigration occurred more recently than it has for some other groups, comparatively fewer vote. As more Indians become citizens, the proportion that is eligible to vote will grow. There are also now a number of Indian-American political action committees.

Learn more

THIS CULTURAL COMPETENCE guide is a short start on all you can learn about Indians in America. We hope you will take things further by talking to people or by using some of these resources. Several of them helped us:

A Part, Yet Apart: South Asians in Asian America, Lavina Shankar, Temple University Press, 1998

American Karma: Race, Culture, and Identity in the Indian Diaspora, Sunil Bhatia, New York University Press, 2007

Asian Indians in Michigan, Arthur W. Helweg, Michigan State University Press, 2002

Bollywood Weddings: Dating, Engagement, and Marriage in Hindu America, Kavita Ramdya, Lexington Books, 2011

Desi Rap: Hip Hop and South Asian America, Ajay Nair, Murali Balaji, Utkarsh Ambudkar (eds.), Lexington Books, 2007

Desis in the House: Indian American Youth Culture In NYC, Sunaina Marr Maira, Temple University Press, 2002

Harbingers of Global Change: India's Techno-Immigrants in the United States, Roli Varma, Rowman & Littlefield, 2006

Leaving India: My Family's Journey from Five Villages to Five Continents, Minal Hajratwala, Houghton Mifflin Harcourt, 2009

New Cosmopolitanisms: South Asians in the U.S., Gita Rajan and Shailja Sharma (eds.), Stanford University Press, 2006

New Roots in America's Sacred Ground: Religion, Race, and Ethnicity in Indian America, Khyati Y. Joshi, Rutgers University Press, 2006

Suburban Sahibs, Mitra Kalita, Rutgers University Press, 2005

Uncle Swami: South Asians in America Today, Vijay Prashad, The New Press, 2012

Unruly Immigrants: Rights, Activism, and Transnational South Asian Politics in the United States, Monisha Das Gupta, Duke University Press, 2006

Work Roles, Gender Roles, and Asian Indian Immigrant Women in the United States, Arpana Sircar, Edwin Mellen Press, 2000

The Story of India, PBS, 360 minutes, 2009

Hidden India: The Kerala Spicelands, PBS, 60 minutes, 2002

∾

We suggest you connect with organizations in your immediate area. These are a few that tend to be more national.

Asian American Convenience Stores Association, *http://www.aacsa.org/FactSheet.php*

Asian American Hotel Owners Association, *http://www.aahoa.com/*

American Teluga Association, *http://www.ataworld.org/*

Association of Kannada Kootas of America, *http://www.akkaonline.com/*

Bichitra, a Bengali Telighious and Cultural Organization, *http://www.bichitra.org/website/*

Bruhan Maharashtra Mahal of North America, *http://www.bmmonline.org/*

Federation of Tamil Sangams of North America, *http:// www.fetna.org/*

GarhamChai.com contains a list of Indian organizations, *http://www.garamchai.com/desiassc.htm*

Hindu American Foundation, *http://www.hafsite.org/*

JAINA: Federation of Jain Associations in North America, *http://www.jaina.org/*

Network of Indian Professionals, *http://na.netip.org/*

Teluga Association of North America, *http://www.tana. org/*

World Sikh Council, America Region, *http://www. worldsikhcouncil.org/*

Websites

Asian Nation
http://www.asian-nation.org

Migration Policy Institute's Information Source
http://www.migrationinformation.org/USfocus/display.
cfm?id=785

Pew Research Center's report on social and demographic trends among Asian Americans
http://www.pewsocialtrends.org/asianamericans/

The Pew Forum on Religion and Public Life
http://www.pewforum.org/global-religious-landscape.
aspx

Real Sikhism: Exploring the Sikh Religion
http://www.realsikhism.com/index.
php?subaction=showfull&id=1248365083&ucat=7

The Smithsonian's Indian American Heritage Project
http://apa.si.edu/indianamerican/

CPSIA information can be obtained at www.ICGtesting.com
Printed in the USA
BVOW08s1904170814

362996BV00008B/29/P